Piano Time Jazz Duets

Book 2

Contents

Pauline Hall

MUSIC DEPARTMENT

OXFORD
UNIVERSITY PRESS

I just want to say . . .

Alan Bullard

Happy and lively

2

I just want to say . . .

Happy and lively

Alan Bullard

Play RH an octave higher.

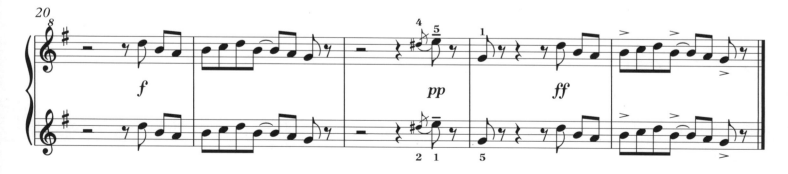

Secondo

Swing's the thing

Alan Haughton

Swing's the thing

Alan Haughton

All I want

Peter Gritton

All I want is a nice ba - na - na . . .

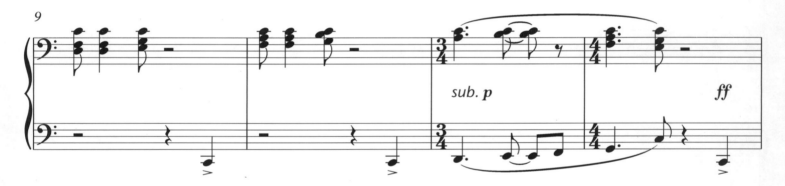

6

All I want

Peter Gritton

All I want is a nice ba - na - na . . .

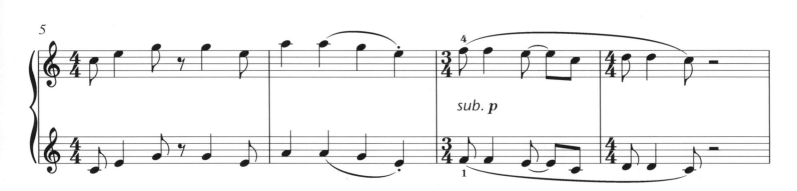

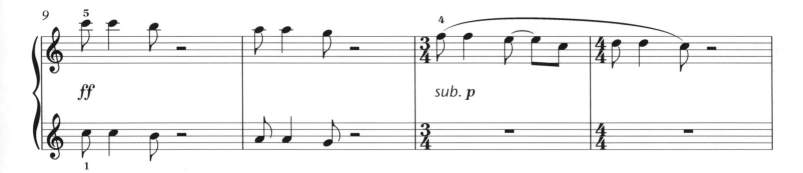

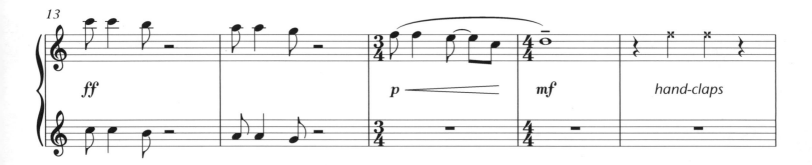

Wrong number

Pauline Hall

Primo

Secondo

It seems to me we're on the wrong wave - length,_____ when -

- ev - er I want to talk to you; and i - ma - gine my frus - tra - tion when there's

no com - mu - ni - ca - tion, ev - en if it's just to say we're through.

Wrong num-ber,___ that's what I al-ways get, the wrong num-ber,___ I some-how seem to get the

wrong num-ber ring-ing when I try to call you.___ If

on-ly I could talk to you I know I'd feel O-K, when you an-swered the phone. You

seem so far a-way, I can't make you un-der-stand what it's like to be a - lone.

Wrong num-ber, it's al-ways just the same, the wrong num-ber,

rall. **slower**

and who's to blame if it's the wrong num-ber ring-ing when I'm miss-ing you!

rall. **slower**

Sassy

Steve Milloy

Dreamy beguine

Denis McCaldin

Relaxed and gently rhythmic

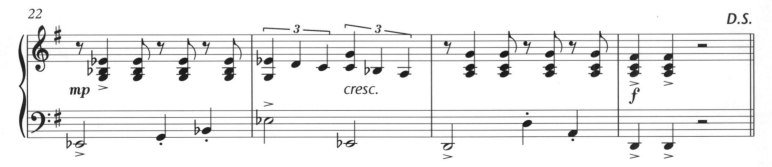

Dreamy beguine

Denis McCaldin

Rags to riches

Alan Haughton

Rags to riches

Alan Haughton

Moonlight waltz

Stephen Duro

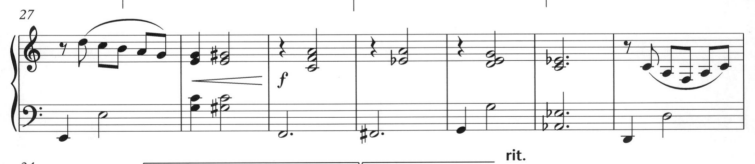

Moonlight waltz

Stephen Duro

Rampage

Charles Beale

Giving it the works!

Stephen Duro

al - le-lu - ia!

al - le-lu - ia!

Slower

loco

Follow the blues

Alan Bullard

Follow the blues

In the first section the right hand *either* copies the left hand (an octave higher) *or* improvises.
In the second section the hands are reversed!

Alan Bullard

Still

Charles Beale

Flowing

p

con Ped.

28

Primo

Charles Beale

Still

Flowing

molto rit.

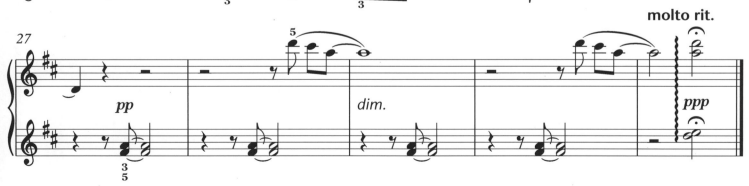

29

The Gambler

Nikki Iles

The Gambler

Nikki Iles

Driving

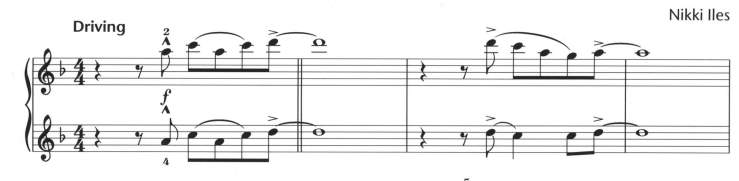

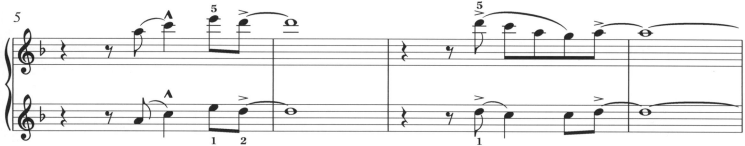

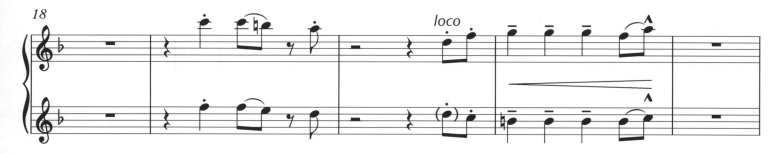

Boogie-woogie-hoogie

This energetic boogie can be played either straight or swung (♫ = ♪³♪)

Roderick Williams

33

Hard cheese

The pupil plays Secondo in this funky duet. The RH melody in bars 13–20 is optional.

Alan Bullard

(RH optional until bar 21)

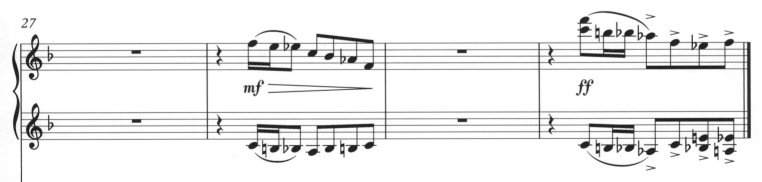

Bossa cinco

Roderick Williams

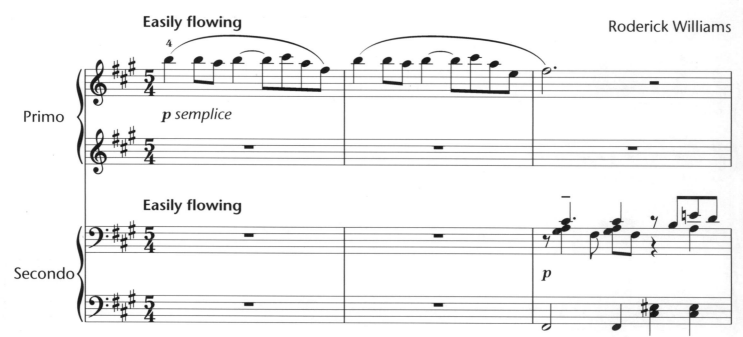